Studies in Preaching 1

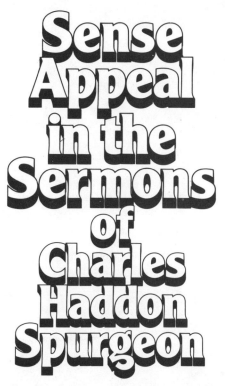

Sense Appeal in the Sermons of Charles Haddon Spurgeon

JAY E. ADAMS

D1564625

BAKER BOOK HOUSE
Grand Rapids, Michigan

Reprinted 1976 by
Baker Book House Company

ISBN: 0-8010-0102-1

First Printing, July 1976
Second Printing, March 1977

PHOTOLITHOPRINTED BY CUSHING - MALLOY, INC.
ANN ARBOR, MICHIGAN, UNITED STATES OF AMERICA
1977

CONTENTS

ABOUT THIS SERIES

With this volume I issue the first in a contemplated series of studies in preaching that I plan to publish from time to time. As currently projected, each of these studies will focus upon one important aspect of one preacher. The series is open-ended. The volumes are designed to help both pastors and seminary students improve their own preaching.

I have begun the series with Charles Haddon Spurgeon because he is so well-loved, and because there is universal agreement that much can be learned from him. I trust that the series will begin to fill a need that I have recognized for some time.

Jay E. Adams
Professor of Practical Theology
Westminster Theological Seminary
Chestnut Hill, Pa.
1975

PREFACE

A number of years ago, when I decided to study some phase of the preaching of Charles Haddon Spurgeon, Andrew W. Blackwood suggested that I analyze his use of Sense Appeal. I followed his suggestion and discovered, to my satisfaction and profit, a wealth of valuable material that I have now determined to share with others. I am convinced that a careful application of the results of this study will help any preacher to improve his preaching greatly. People heard Spurgeon gladly. One reason was his welcome use of Sense Appeal.

The procedure that I have adopted follows a logical order. Beginning with an analysis of the sermons themselves. I adduce proof of the existence of a significant amount of Sense Appeal in them. If this cannot be established, the entire purpose of the book is defeated. Therefore, it seemed to be the proper starting point. Once assembled, these data became the raw material for developing criteria by which to evaluate the testimony of commentators, which thus used constituted an additional body of evidence for the existence of Sense Appeal.

The next step was to determine whether the power of Sense Appeal is a worthwhile and attainable goal for which others might strive. This led to a discussion of the origin of Spurgeon's ability. Did it flow from some innate genius? If so, the study would have proved to be of little practical value to non-geniuses. At best, its results could stand only as a warning for them not to attempt the impossible. Was it acquired by hard work and conscious effort? If so, the practical value of the fact is obvious. I concluded from Spurgeon's own testimony as well as that of others that the latter was primarily the case. That led to the final task: to analyze and classify the data at hand, abstracting the principles involved in the techniques of Sense Appeal, and putting these into systematic form. This done, the work was concluded.

I must note that the procedure outlined above omits all reference to God's grace in the acquisition and use of Sense Appeal in the sermons in question. Far from denying either its existence or importance, I assume it everywhere. But since man looks on the outward appearance, and only God can look upon the heart, I have had to settle for what God has allowed me to do. Therefore, I have delimited my study to encompass only the observable human aspects that are involved.

INTRODUCTION

The investigation of any aspect of the life, ministry, or preaching of Charles Haddon Spurgeon hardly needs justification. His immense stature as a preacher is well known. Since he towered above all of the great preachers of his age, his theory and methods of preaching warrant specialized study. Blackwood's words well summarize the all but universal evaluation of this many-sided man:

> In more recent times Charles Haddon Spurgeon (1834-92) became probably the most influential pastoral preacher since the days of the Apostles. According to the late Sir William Robertson Nicholl, editor of *The British Weekly,* and a learned bookman, every young minister in the English-speaking world ought to saturate his soul in the sermons of Spurgeon, and thus learn the secrets of a soul-winning and life-building ministry.[1]

He further says,

> The sermons ought to whet the desire to learn the facts of Spurgeon's career, and the secret of his power. To many of us he seems the mightiest preacher in Christendom since the Apostle Paul.[2]

The extent and duration of his success not only warrants but demands analysis. For over forty years he consistently attracted capacity crowds in England's largest auditoriums. His printed sermons, translated into many languages, girdled the globe. His philanthropic works included an orphanage and a seminary. Today, his writings are still studied by thousands. No wonder Brown

---

[1]A. W. Blackwood, *Preaching From the Bible,* p. 27. New York: Abingdon-Cokesbury Press, 1941.
[2]*Ibid.,* p. 9.

declared, "He is worthy of prolonged and careful study on the part of every preacher.[3]

However, it was not the mere curiosity of uncovering the secret behind a phenomenal success story that motivated this study. Rather, I had but one overriding thought in mind. I wanted to discover the ways and means by which Spurgeon appealed to the senses, in order that those principles might be summarized and used by others.[4] Thus, this study is at once both narrow and practical.

Any serious study of Spurgeon's preaching is sure to yield much profit. However, since he bequeathed it to us in such abundance it is a physical impossibility for one to survey the whole of his preaching from all aspects.[5] I have considered it proper, therefore, to choose but one distinguishing feature for this investigation.

One fact that even the most casual student of Spurgeon recognizes is his complete mastery of and intimate familiarity with the best preachers and religious authors prior to his time. In his day, he was probably the most able student of the Puritan literature.[6] He read the Puritan writers, wrote about them,[7] and adopted their style as his own. Brastow, who calls him "The Puritan Pastoral Evangelist," says, "he was. . . incessantly occupied in reading."[8] At the age of fourteen he went to live with his grandfather, James Spurgeon, who was the pastor of an Independent church, and an enthusiastic Calvinist.[9] It was here that he came to know and love the old volumes to which he later fell heir. Needham reports, "directed by the venerable pastor, he soon developed into the thoughtful boy,

---

[3]John Brown, *Puritan Preaching in England,* p. 226. New York: Charles Scribner's Sons, 1900.
[4]*Infra.,* Chap. VII.
[5]Although the exact number is unknown, the total of printed sermons is well in excess of 2,000.
[6]Louis O. Brastow, *Representative Modern Preachers,* p. 388. New York: Hodder and Stoughton, 1904.
[7]See especially the following books by Spurgeon: *Commenting and Commentators, The Art of Illustration, The Treasure of David,* and *Illustrations and Meditations.*
[8]Brastow, *op. cit.,* p. 53. One who knew him at the age of sixteen wrote: "He was a smart, clever boy at all kinds of book learning." H. L. Wayland, *Charles H. Spurgeon: His Faith and Works,* p. 14. Philadelphia: American Baptist Publication Society, 1892
[9]Wayland, *op. cit.,* p. 10.

fonder of his book than of his play.[10] But he was no slave to the Puritans. He milked them dry, but he made his own butter.[11]

It would seem, therefore, that Spurgeon himself is one of the finest illustrations of the value of the careful study of preaching. Thus, his own example encouraged me to make the study that lies behind this book.

The absence of any contemporary pastoral preacher even remotely as effective as Spurgeon, indicates a present need for his kind of preaching. Perhaps, when you have completed this book, you will agree that one of the failures of modern preaching is the lack of that sort of Sense Appeal which so characterized Spurgeon's sermons. This is particularly so in an age in which so many persons have learned to develop their capacity for right brain learning (visual-emotive learning) through the influence of television. That such appeal was popular before the advent of TV is certain from the ministry of Spurgeon himself. But today, it seems essential since there is so little development of the rational capacities.

Until every aspect of his preaching is dissected, analyzed, and systematized according to its theoretical principles and practices (as this study attempts to do with respect to one aspect) the Spurgeon phenomenon will make little practical impact upon present day preaching. The fact that no analysis of this aspect of Spurgeon's sermons is available[12] also indicated that such a study would afford an opportunity to make an original and worthwhile contribution to the accumulating Spurgeon literature.

Finally, the significant influence of Sense Appeal in Spurgeon's sermons is demonstrated by the testimony of readers and hearers whose statements and estimates are adduced as evidence in Chapter Four, and, therefore, need not be reiterated here.

---

[10]George C. Needham, *Charles H. Spurgeon, His Life and Labors,* p. 29. Manchester: Albert Needham, Publisher, 1890.

[11]For example, Spurgeon never was caught up in the harmful preparationist views of that strain of Puritanism that brought such havoc into Calvinistic circles by introducing Arminian, Roman Catholic congruism under the guise of Calvinism.

[12]This is virgin study. The standard catalogues offer no literature specifically devoted to this matter.

CHAPTER ONE
SENSE APPEAL

This book is limited to the discussion of one element[1] in Charles H. Spurgeon's sermons and one element alone: Sense Appeal. Its purpose is to demonstrate the existence of Sense Appeal in Spurgeon's preaching to such an extent and of such a quality as to make it noteworthy. I have sought to illuminate the composition and structure of this appeal in such a way that by formulating principles, I might make Spurgeon's theory and practice accessible to others. Style in general, biographical data, and the variegated aspects of the ministry of this unusual man were by-passed entirely. They were beyond the scope of this monograph.

I do wish to make one thing clear however: it is neither the thesis of this book nor the conclusion of my research that Spurgeon's success as a pastoral preacher might be attributed either wholly or even primarily to his remarkable ability to appeal to the senses of his listeners. To aver such, would be misleading. It would necessitate such narrowness of viewpoint as to blind one to the many other significant qualities in his life, e.g., personality, and sermons. Such a conclusion could be reached only by magnifying the value of the present study to undue proportions, a temptation to which one who has worked so closely with it might easily succumb. Perhaps Spurgeon's brother most accurately described the major factor in the great preacher's success when he said, "I think that it lies in the fact that he loves Jesus of Nazareth and Jesus of Nazareth loves

---

[1]Except as others relate to the present thesis. For example, Spurgeon's use of illustrations had to be studied carefully, because illustrative material and Sense Appeal are often so closely associated, and because in Spurgeon's book, *The Art of Illustration*, certain principles reveal his philosophy concerning Sense Appeal as it pertains to illustration. Such biographical information as sheds light upon the origin of his method of Sense Appeal also was necessarily included. But little else.

him."[2] Beyond everything else, we must see this as primary. Those who seek to emulate him, therefore, should begin by following the example of his devotion to Christ. Otherwise, imitation of his use of Sense Appeal (or anything else) will take the form of the imitation of tricks and gimmicks.

Yet, to set the present study in proper perspective to Spurgeon's preaching as a whole, and the fundamental causes of his success before God, in no way minimizes its vital importance. The other (more) important factors would have suffered considerably apart from it. It was the wrapper in which he presented the precious gospel product. Though it added nothing to the product itself, it was fitting to it, and did not detract from but rather complemented it. Without it, it is safe to say that the "prince of preachers"[3] would have been something less than that.

The research in primary sermon sources[4] was purposely limited to the twenty volume set of sermons comprising the *Memorial Library*,[5] that contains a total of four hundred twenty-five sermons in all. Each of these, including the one volume life of Spurgeon by Pike, was analyzed (some were studied more thoroughly than others because of the presence or lack of various qualities) in preparing this work.[6]

This limitation was set for several reasons. The first was availability. The *Memorial Library* more readily brought together a wide variety of sermons. Four hundred twenty-five sermons, selected from Spurgeon's entire forty-odd year ministry seemed to provide a better cross section than volumes published at particular intervals during that time. Moreover, I considered the laborious task of reading and evaluating material found in four hundred twenty-five sermons the physical maximum. Since the printed

---

[2]Quoted in Jesse Page, *C. H. Spurgeon, His Life and Ministry*, p. vi. New York: Fleming H. Revell, n.d.

[3]*Ibid.*, p. vii.

[4]Other primary sources were used (see the bibliography), but only these sermon sources.

[5]C. H. Spurgeon, *Spurgeon's Sermons, The Memorial Library*. New York: Funk and Wagnalls Co., n.d. All footnote references to sermons hereafter will be cited by volume and page number, and will refer to the *Memorial Library* unless otherwise noted.

[6]The method of study is demonstrated in a somewhat more detailed manner in Appendix I by an analysis of one sermon.

sermons number in the thousands, some arbitrary number had to be set, and the *Memorial Library,* as the most compact unit of sermons available, together with the reasons above, seemed to provide the least arbitrary limitation possible.

Definition

I should take a moment to explain my title, *Sense Appeal*. Sense Appeal as I have used it in this study means the technique employed in preaching to activate the five senses without the use of objective sense stimuli.

By "preaching" is meant primarily the particular written sermons of Spurgeon as delimited above.

CHAPTER TWO
SENSE APPEAL
IN SPURGEON'S SERMONS

I remember the hour when I stepped into a little place of worship, and saw a tall thin man step into the pulpit. . . . He opened the Bible and read, with a feeble voice, "Look unto me, and be ye saved all the ends of the earth. . . ." Ah, thought I, I am one of the ends of the earth; and then turning round, and fixing his gaze on me, as if he knew me, the minister said, "Look, look, look."[1]

This is Spurgeon's own account of his conversion.[2] He never forgot it. He loved to recall it in his sermons. Why? It was the turning point in his life. But note too—that Primitive Methodist sermon contained Sense Appeal *par excellence*. In it, the minister drew a word picture of the Saviour on the cross. He then directly appealed to the sense of sight so strongly through the repetitive use of the word "look" that Spurgeon says, "I looked that moment."[3] The text gave the clue, and the preacher used it to the fullest extent. It was that element of the sermon that Spurgeon emphasized whenever he recalled the event.

It is evident that the deep impression that this sermon made upon Spurgeon remained; this is so especially with respect to the direct use of Sense Appeal.[4] In a message on the same text (that is heavily

---

[1]Vol. 1, p. 319.

[2]Elsewhere, he adds this further information: "Just setting his eyes upon me, as if he knew me by heart, he said, 'Young man, you are in trouble.' Well I was sure enough. Says he, 'You will never get out of it unless you look to Christ.' " George C. Lorimer, *Charles Haddon Spurgeon, The Puritan Preacher*, p. 31. Boston: James H. Earle, publisher, 1892.

[3]Vo. 1, p. 1.

[4]Spurgeon commented, "Oh, I looked until I could almost have looked my eyes away, and in Heaven I will look on still in my joy unutterable." Lorimer, *op. cit.*, p. 31.

reminiscent of it), Spurgeon himself employed Sense Appeal to advantage. He appealed to the sense of taste:

> Have we not seen our God dash the goblet to the earth, spill the sweet wine, and instead thereof fill it with gall?... Drain the cup and know its bitterness... nauseous the draught was.[5]

He appealed also to the hearing: "I hear a shout, 'Look and be saved.' "[6] And at the climax of the sermon, he drew a great word picture appealing to the sight:

> From the cross of Calvary, where the bleeding hands of Jesus drop mercy; from the garden of Gethsemane, where the bleeding pores of the Saviour sweat pardons, the cry comes, "Look unto me, and be ye saved..." look thou there....Those hands were nailed for thee; those feet gushed gore for thee, that side was opened wide for thee; and if thou wantest to know how thou canst find mercy, there it is "Look!"[7]

Prior to analyzing any additional quotations, I should like to distinguish between what may be called *direct* and *indirect* Sense Appeal. The former may be defined as a direct summons to the hearer to exercise one or more of his senses, as, for example in the above quotation when Spurgeon said, "look thou there." The latter is an indirect stimulation of the senses by means of word-description. A vivid illustration of indirect appeal to the sight is found in the phrase, "the bleeding pores of the Saviour sweat pardons." Direct appeal in Spurgeon almost always involves a command or interrogation, whereas indirect appeal is descriptive in nature. Both are effectively employed by him throughout his sermons.

One unique feature of Spurgeon's appeal to the senses was his wide use of the direct method. While there is some indirect appeal (although far too little) in present day preaching, there seems to be

---

[5]Vol. 1, p. 10.
[6]Vol. 1, p. 14.
[7]Vol. 1, pp. 14-15.

very little direct appeal. Some ministers may preach a lifetime and never use it. Direct appeal is more authoritative, and demands not only a certain amount of dogmatism, but a kind of courage and boldness that does not characterize the temper of most contemporary sermons. But Spurgeon urged his students, "Do not deliver your message with bated breath. Tell it out boldly."[8]

This direct appeal to the senses may be discerned in the following sampling of imperatives that are sprinkled unsparingly throughout all his sermons: "See, Behold, Mark, Admire, Look, Observe, Turn your eyes, View, Hear, Listen, Hearken, Drink, Taste."

While it is of special interest to take note of direct appeal wherever it occurs because of its unique quality, nevertheless we shall be concerned with indirect appeal as well.

Next, something must be said of the ratios between the appeal to each of the senses. It was impossible to determine such ratios with any kind of mathematical precision for two reasons: First, the human equation was an insurmountable problem. What one reviewer may believe to be an instance of Sense Appeal, another may not. This is true especially of indirect appeal. While all will agree upon clear-cut passages such as those quoted above, there are many that are not quite so clear. Secondly, in many places the appeal to two or more senses was bound together so inextricably that it was impossible to distinguish between them. Therefore, all ratios had to be of a very general nature. But for what they are worth, subjective as they are, I shall share my conclusions with you.

It was found, as expected, that the instances of sight appeal rated far above all others, and, indeed, occurred more often than all of the rest of the appeals combined. In this, Spurgeon was like other preachers (although this use of indirect and direct appeal to sight probably outweighs most others). The appeal to hearing was unusually frequent, occurring more often than the three remaining senses together. This too was expected from early readings. The last three,[9] however, remained uncertain at the outset of the investiga-

---

[8]*An All-Round Ministry*, p. 35. London: Passmore and Alabaster, 1900. Page says, "It is clear that Spurgeon practised the teaching which he was never tired of giving to his students as to being *direct* in their appeals." *C. H. Spurgeon, His Life and Ministry*, p. 88. New York: Fleming H. Revell, n.d.

[9]Spurgeon is exceptional in that he departs from the pattern of most preachers who confine their Sense Appeal to the senses of sight and hearing. In this, he even excells Bunyan, who spoke almost exclusively of the "Eye-gate" and "Ear-gate."

tion, and, therefore, were a matter of much interest to me. Here were my results: while the appeal to smell and taste vied closely for last place (so closely it would be difficult to say accurately which was the more frequent); surprisingly,[10] the appeal to touch occurred as often as these two taken together.

---

[10]The writer expected to find Taste Appeal in third place. It is his conjecture (after a good bit of reflection) that Spurgeon's rigid, almost vegetarian diet may have dulled his sense of taste (thus affecting his preaching appeal to this sense). W. I. Hatcher writes, "He had to guard against anything that would tend to fatten him and he used 'saccharine' instead of sugar for sweetening his coffee. His pleasures in eating were narrowly limited." In Wayland, *op. cit.*, p. 189.

CHAPTER THREE
APPEAL TO THE SIGHT

Turning to actual quotations selected from Spurgeon's sermons, we shall consider these categorically under the head of each of the five senses, beginning with Sight Appeal.

Spurgeon consciously labored to paint word-pictures for his hearers. Interestingly enough, he was not averse to disclose the fact, even in the sermons themselves. Here are two such passages:

> If anyone of us could, in our inmost souls, behold that scene, should we not be overcome? I wish I could so speak this morning that some of you would picture that last tremendous day, for which all other days were made. . . . Behold it by anticipation.[1]

In that quotation, it is not difficult to see the preacher struggling to paint what is beyond his grasp. In another place, speaking of the death of Christ he urged the listener also to get involved in the process of mind painting.

> Painful as the picture is, it will do you good to paint it. You will need neither canvas, nor brush, nor pallette, nor colors. Let your thoughts draw the outline, your love fill in the detail; I shall not complain if imagination heightens the coloring.[2]

Both quotations indicate the clearest sort of conscious intention to appeal to the sight. In them, Spurgeon not only does make such an appeal, but talks about doing so. He spoke often in this vein, directly calling upon his hearer to exercise his imagination; using what, in

---

[1]Vol. 19, p. 262.
[2]Vol. 19, p. 212.

one sermon, he terms "the eyes of the mind,"[3] and in another, the "spiritual eyes."[4] Either of these expressions (but especially the first) might serve well as defining synonyms for "Sight Appeal," as I have used this expression. Spurgeon, it seems, firmly believed that the mind could "see" word-pictures as readily with its "spiritual eyes" as the body sees with its physical eyes. This conviction squarely underlaid his theory of preaching. Constantly, therefore, he demanded that his listeners open their eyes and see what he had to show them from God. This, incidentally, indicates that he saw preaching as a cooperative enterprise in which not only the preacher, but also the listener is an active participant. In this he was far ahead of his times.

His attitude seemed to be that listeners who failed to use the "eyes of the mind" were as culpable as those who had shut their physical eyes to that which they were obligated to see. He himself "saw" so vividly, that sometimes he seemed a bit impatient with others whose mental eyesight was deficient. For example, listen to him as he tried to persuade people to open their eyes to spiritual scenes: "Do you mark him in your imagination nailed to yonder cross! Do you see his hands bleeding, and his feet gushing gore? Behold him!"[5] Again, "Do you see him?.... Look at him!... see him! See him!"[4] Preaching about the mighty deeds of God's servants, he concluded the paragraph this way: "Can you not realize these as literal facts? Do they stand up in all their brightness before your eyes?"[6]

But he could not only summon his hearers to open their eyes, he did all that he could to help them do so. By vivid realistic description, he hung living word-paintings before them, indirectly appealing to their sense of sight; enabling them to employ this God-given capacity to see with the eyes of their minds. Living, vibrant description poured forth from his lips. There follow only the most meager samplings from an unfathomable mine of possible

[3]Vol. 19, p. 31.
[4]Vol. 19, p. 195.
[5]Vol. 2, p. 144.
[5]Vol. 2, p. 148. Here he is in a struggle with the listener, urging, pleading, helping him to open the eyes of his soul and *see*.
[6]Vol. 6, p. 24.

quotations. One excells the next in beauty, realism and other fine descriptive qualities. Each quotation has been selected because it represents clearly and unmistakably what is meant in this paper by "Sense Appeal" to the sight. Some are direct appeal; others are indirect. Some are thumbnail sketches; others are more detailed pictures. Some are blacks and whites; others are painted in the most colorful oils. The very fact of such variety, shows the hand of the master, to whom every art medium was the same.

To begin with, take a look at some of his brief charcoal sketches: Instead of prosaicly stating that there will be no new revelation beyond the pages of the Scriptures, Spurgeon declared, "When it has been forgotten, and laid in the dusty chamber of our memory, he fetches it out and cleans the picture, but does not paint a new one."[7] When his subject was the iniquity of the human heart, he described it as a volcano that even "when it belches not forth its lava, and sendeth not forth the hot stones of its corruption, is still the same dread volcano."[8] Rather than abstractly state the fact that Christ was tempted to the fullest extent (as most modern preachers would), Spurgeon cried, "Not an arrow out of the quiver of hell was spared; the whole were shot against him."[9] Beautifully, he described the death of the Christian: "the Lord puts his finger upon your eyelids and kisses your soul out at your lips."[10] Referring to the text, "The word is nigh thee, even in thy mouth," he explained: "When a morsel is in your mouth, if you desire to possess it so as never to lose it, what is the best thing to do? Swallow it."[11] For the quality of sheer beauty itself, consider the following sentence: "the dew-drops glisten like tears, standing in the eyes of the flowers, as if they wept for joy to see the sun again after the long night of darkness."[12] How did he plead for faith? Constantly he reechoed the word of his own conversion, "Look," but he was by no means shut up to this one expression. Here

[7]Vol. 1, p. 79.
[8]Vol. 1, p. 241.
[9]Vol. 6, p. 153. This is an excellent example of Spurgeon's usual method of teaching Christian doctrine. He had the ability to "make doctrinal preaching shine." Notes from Blackwood's courses in 1957.
[10]Vol. 5, p. 287.
[11]Vol. 14, p. 339. Also an appeal to the sense of taste.
[12]Vol. 6, p. 249.

is a figure for faith that because of its very simplicity and candor was extremely bold: "Wilt thou drop into his arms, and let him carry thee?"[13] To describe the elimination of all weariness in heaven, he employed this unusual imagery from the realm of nature: "O, how blessed to flap the wing forever, and never feel it flag."[14] One reads of "prayers that rise like mountains,"[15] and the "golden sands of life" dropping "unheeded from the hourglass."[16] Judgment day was described colorfully: "the sea is boiling" and "the waves are lit up with supernatural splendour."[17] Slothful Christians were told: "the Devil is grinning at thy sleepy face; sleeping while demons are dancing round thy slumbering carcass, and telling it in hell that a Christian is asleep."[18] Unsettled conditions were likened to birdlife: "the great majority of mankind are always on the wing; they never settle: they never light on any tree to build their nest."[19] He spoke of "the wine of self-satisfaction, around the brim" of which "you may see the bubbles of pride."[20] And "unbelief," he declared, "hath more phases than the moon, and more colors than the chameleon."[21] Cain's guilt was personified as "a grim chamberlain, with fingers bloody red" drawing "the curtain of his bed each night."[22] The law, he said, "is Sarah's handmaid to sweep our hearts, and make the dust fly so hard that we may cry for blood to be sprinkled that the dust may be laid."[23] The value of persecution was described nautically: "Christ's church never sails so well as when she is rocked from side to side by the winds of persecution; when the spray of her blood dashes in the front, and when she is wellnigh overwhelmed."[24] Creation was pictured impressively: "like drops of dew from the fingers of the morning, stars and constellations fell trickling from the hands of God . . . by his own lips, he launched

---

[13]Vol. 4, p. 110.
[14]Vol. 3, p. 142. Note also the reoccurring "f."
[15]Vol. 2, p. 204.
[16]Vol. 2, p. 36.
[17]Vol. 2, p. 64.
[18]Vol. 1, p. 355.
[19]Vol. 2, p. 40.
[20]Vol. 5, p. 277.
[21]Vol. 2, p. 52.
[22]Vol. 5, p. 75.
[23]Vol. 2, p. 123.
[24]Vol. 2, p. 157.

forth ponderous orbs . . . he sent the comet, like thunderbolts, wandering through the sky."[25] It is important to observe that many of the pictures above are not still life, but moving pictures, characterized by action. Another such, clearly illustrating this same quality of animation follows:

> Death is riding! Here his horse comes—I hear his snortings, I feel his hot breath—he comes! And thou must die![26]

The host of Israelites crossing the sea was pictured this way: "Look yonder. . . . Lo, they tred the pebbly bottom of the sea of Edom, while the waters stand like walls of snow-white crystal on the right and on the left."[27]

So much for these samplings of the type of brief word-sketches with which Spurgeon's sermons were studded. He was the master of detailed painting as well. Here are two fine passages. The first is typical of those found in many of his sermons since he was fond of portraying the cross (the central theme of all of his preaching):

> But look thou here—seest thou that man hanging on the cross? Dost thou behold his agonized head dropping meekly down upon his breast? Dost thou see that thorny crown, causing drops of blood to trickle down his cheeks? Dost thou see his hands pierced and rent, and his blest feet supporting the weight of his own frame, rent well-nigh in twain with the cruel nails? Sinner! dost thou hear him shriek, "Eloi, eloi, lama sabbacthani?" Dost thou hear him cry, "It is finished?" Dost thou mark his head hang down in death? Seest thou that side pierced with the spear, and the body taken from the cross? O come thou hither![28]

The second gave assurance of the firm basis for patient trust in God's providence during times of trial:

> If we were to deal with the weather with the same short-sighted doubt which governs us in our thoughts of divine providence, we might be doubtful about summer and winter. We might say, "It really does not look very likely that spring will come. Look at the meadows, and mark how the cold has literally burned the

---

[25]Vol. 2, p. 78.
[26]Vol. 2, p. 216. Note also the appeals to the senses of hearing and feeling.
[27]Vol. 2, p. 155. Hearing also is appealed to.
[28]Vol. 1, p. 15.

grass; see how our hardy evergreens are many of them dead, and others sadly cut to pieces; see what mischief the cold has wrought. Will there ever be leaf and flower again? Is it possible that I shall ever wipe the sweat from my smoking brow on some blazing noontide? Can these frozen brooks leap into liberty? Today we crowd around the fire, hardly keeping ourselves alive from the bitter cold; shall we yet bask in the hay-field, or fan ourselves amid the golden sheaves?" Had we less experience, it would seem highly improbable. Yet we enjoy a full assurance as to the revolution of the seasons and the succession of day and night; do we not? Why this assurance of the one promise, and why such frequent distrusts of others equally true?[29]

Both clearly paint pictures. The first used descriptive indirect appeal in combination with direct questions, while the second was almost entirely indirect in approach. Such descriptions abound.

But Spurgeon was a master artist who was not afraid to lay aside his brush and canvas and even try his hand at word sculpture! How many preachers would have dared this? Here is the remarkable passage (found in a sermon with the kinesthetic sense-appealing topic, "Hands Full of Honey"):

I have before now met with that popular artist Gustave Dore and suggested subjects to him. Had he survived among us, and had another opportunity occurred, I would have pressed him to execute a statue of Samson handing out the honey: strength distributing sweetness; and it might have served as a perpetual reminder of what a Christian should be—a Conqueror and a Comforter, slaying lions and distributing honey. . . . Set the statue before your mind's eye, and now let me speak about it.[30]

This he proceeded to do, very effectively.

It should be evident from the above quotations that Spurgeon made abundant use of eye appeal. It was prominent in every sermon, *without exception*. It stands as *the outstanding* trademark of a Spurgeon sermon.

CHAPTER FOUR
APPEAL TO THE HEARING

Others have excelled in appealing to the sight; perhaps none so effectively as Spurgeon. Few, however have ventured into the realms of other senses. Spurgeon did. Second only to sight appeal was his appeal to hearing. Many of the passages in which such appeal occurs have to do with song and include a reference to the human voice. Only secondarily does Spurgeon's appeal to sound stem from the vibrations of nature. Sometimes the sounds are pleasing; sometimes discordant. Often, as in the appeal to the eye, the approach is direct. Here are some samples of each variety. The first is an example of direct appeal and is cited by Needham, who explains:

> Speaking of those who are so well satisfied with themselves and with their surroundings that they refuse to bow to the authority of God, he shouted, "You will not glorify him? You will not glorify him?" Then, dropping his voice to a low and thrilling tone, he said, "Yes, you will, and you shall. I tell you the groans of the damned in hell are the deep bass of the universal anthem of praise that shall ascend to the throne of my God for ever and ever!"[1]

More frequently, the appeal is indirect as in the following examples:

> If we were to cease to sing his praise, would Jesus Christ's name be forgotten then? No; the stones would sing, the hills would be an orchestra, the mountains would skip like rams. . . . Why, the sun would lead the chorus; the moon would play upon her silver harp, and sweetly sing to her music; stars would dance in their measured courses; the shoreless depths of ether would become the home of songs, and the void immensity would burst out into

---

[1]*Op. cit.,* p. 13.

one great shout. . . . Can Christ's name be forgotten? No. . . the winds whisper it; the tempests howl it; the seas chant it;. . . the beasts low it; the thunders proclaim it; earth shouts it; heaven echoes it.[2]

Speaking of the sound of a friend's words, he said,

His words are music. . . . I catch the intonation of each syllable as it falls, for it is like the harmony of the harps of heaven. Oh! there is a voice in love; it speaks a language which is its own.[3]

Mostly, the two were intermingled as in this passage:

Many voices clamor for our attention. . . all call to us and entreat us to hearken, but the Father says, "Hear him. . . ." If Jesus were dead and his prophetic office extinct we might hear others; but since he liveth, we hear the celestial voice rolling along the ages and distinctly crying. "Hear ye him. . . ." Oh, to be content with hearing Christ, and letting other voices go away into the eternal silence.[4]

Often the appeal to sight and hearing were closely joined. Whenever this occurred the usual order was first sight, then hearing. He first sketched the scene from a distance, then brought the listener nearer so that he might hear what was said. Sometimes, however, the purpose was to enable him to touch, or smell, or taste the object in view. But almost always, sight preceded the other senses. Here is a sample of one such sight/sound combination:

The angel, binding you hand and foot, holds you one single moment over the mouth of the chasm. He bids you look down— down—down. There is no bottom; [thus far, sight appeal; now the ear is activated] and you hear coming up from the abyss, sullen moans and hollow groans, and screams of tortured ghosts. [Now both become inter-twined.] You quiver, your bones melt like wax, and your marrow quakes within you. Where is now thy might? And where is thy boasting and bragging? Ye shriek and cry, ye beg for mercy; but the angel,

---

[2]Vol. 1, pp. 163-164.
[3]Vol. 1, p. 73.
[4]Vol. 14, p. 284.

with one tremendous grasp, seizes you fast, and hurls you down, with the cry, "Away, away!" And down you go to the pit that is bottomless, and roll forever downward—downward—downward—ne'er to find a resting place for the soles of your feet. Ye shall be cast out.[5]

Almost all hearing appeal was pleasant or unpleasant, with very little of a merely neutral sort. Not a few passages (like the one above) had to do with the sounds of hell. These are typical excerpts:

When the damned jingle the burning irons of their torments, they shall say "forever."[6]

Thy everlasting yelling in torment cannot move the heart of God; thy groans and briny tears cannot move him to pity thee.[7]

Other discordant or unpleasant sounds are heard:

But do you hear, in the distance, the growling of the thunders of calumny and scorn?[8]

Our hearts like muffled drums, are beating funeral marches to the tomb.[9]

I might hang the world in mourning; I might make the sea the great chief mourner, with its dirge of howling winds, and its wild death-march of disordered waves. . . . I would bid hurricanes howl the solemn wailing—that death-shriek of a world—for what would become of us if we should lose the gospel?[10]

But all is not unpleasant. There are some melodious appeals as well:

Hark! Hark! Methought I heard sweet music; methought I heard a song descending from the regions up above, born down by gales whose breath is sweet as that which comes from the spicy groves of Araby. (A favorite appeal to the sense of smell.) I

---

[5]Vol. 1, pp. 313-314. Another may be cited: *"behold* a Moffat go with the Word of God in his hand, *hear* him preach as the Spirit gives him utterance." Vol. 1, p. 120.
[6]Vol. 1, p. 190.
[7]Vol. 6, p. 30.
[8]Vol. 2, p. 144.
[9]Vol. 1, p. 38.
[10]Vol. 1, p. 161.

heard a sound not earthly. . . . O river of harmony! where are the lips from which thou flowest?[11]

They cannot now talk the brogue of Canaan, nor speak the language of Zion, but they shall do it soon.[12]

The Father calleth us every day with the loud voice of his Son's wounds.[13]

Hark! Across the waves of the Atlantic and the Pacific I hear the sound of prayer and praise from many a vessel bearing the British flag. From many an islet of the sea the song is borne upon the breeze. . . and when England ceases her strain of joy, in the hush of night, Australia takes up the song.[14]

Sometimes, appeal to the hearing was made through dialogue. Here are portions of one such dialogue:

Picture the case of the prodigal son when he went home. Suppose when he reached the house the elder brother had come to meet him. I must take a supposition that the elder brother had sweetened himself, and made himself amiable; and then I hear him say, "Come in, brother, welcome home!" But I see the returning one stand there with the tears in his eyes, and I hear him lament, "I want to see my father. I must tell him that I have sinned and done evil in his sight." An old servant whispers, "Master John, I am glad to see you back. Be happy, for all the servants are rejoiced to hear the sound of your voice. It is true your father will not see you, but he has ordered the fatted calf to be killed for you, and here is the best robe, and a ring, and shoes for your feet, and we are told to put them upon you." All this would not content the poor penitent. I think I hear him cry—"I do not despise anything my father gives me, for I am not worthy to be as his hired servant; but what is all this unless I see his face, and know that he forgives me?[15]

The dialogue method is most effective for creating auditory appeal.

11Vol. 2, p. 165.
12Vol. 3, p. 126.
13Vol. 8, p. 30.
14Vol. 8, pp. 142-143.
15Vol. 14, p. 169.

It is a form that makes the bold use of direct discourse possible. In the above passage, three persons were represented as speaking. With proper control of voice inflection, such as Spurgeon possessed, one could have been made to feel as if he were listening to the actual conversation itself. This was especially true when combined with the descriptive qualities of sight appeal for which he had so great potential.

It is clear, from the evidence, that Spurgeon strongly appealed to the sense of hearing, as well as the sight. What of the other three senses? In the chapter that follows, I shall consider them together.

CHAPTER FIVE
APPEAL TO THE OTHER SENSES

As previously noted, the appeal to the three remaining senses was not so frequent as that of the first two, sight and sound. However, it was sufficiently significant to consider.

Sense of Touch

The sense of feeling (kinesthetic sense, or sense of touch) includes many things. It may be activated by temperatures, hot or cold to the touch; consistencies, hard, soft, wet or dry; textures, rough or smooth; or sensations like pain. These can be external to the body or internal. Spurgeon regularly preached with such appeal:

> Out with your finger! Dear soul, out with your finger! Do not go away till you have touched the Lord by a believing prayer or hope.[1]

Several other passages, specifically including the word "touch" itself may be cited:

> The blind man he touched and gave his sight, and the dead maiden was thus revived. Oh, the power of his touch! Our touch of Jesus saves us; what will not his touch of us do?[2]

> If I were touched by electricity, could I tell whether I was or not? I suppose I should; the shock would be strong enough to make me know where I stood.[3]

> Take Jesus at once, if not with a hand's grasp, yet with a finger's touch.[4]

---

[1]Vol. 19, p. 121.
[2]Vol. 14, p. 288.
[3]Vol. 1, p. 60.
[4]Vol. 19, p. 118.

But some were of other kinds, indicating different tactile and bodily sensations. Inward conviction of heart was represented as "the hand of the Holy Spirit on his soul."[5] One problem of fishing for men was likened to a difficulty in ordinary fishing which graphically involves certain vivid touch sensations:

> The heart is very slippery. Yes! The heart is a fish that troubles all gospel fishermen to hold. . . slimy as an eel, it slippeth between your fingers.[6]

Human reaction to the pain of a thorn-prick was suggested this way:

> The table is daintily spread; the manna of heaven lies close to our hand, but, because there is a little rent in the garment, or a small thorn in the finger, we sit down and cry as though the worst of ills had happened to us![7]

The death of an unsaved man was described in terms of touch appeal and bodily sensation:

> He shuts his eyes, but he feels the cold and bony hand upon his forehead; he quivers, for the sting of death is in his heart.[8]

In speaking of human rebelliousness, he said, "Oh foolish fingers, which prepare prickles for our own pillows!"[9] It may be noted that for the most part, references to kinesthetic appeal were brief. This was found generally to be true concerning all of the last three senses. Since the relative frequency of appeal was considerably less than that of the two former senses, the citations under these heads are naturally fewer in number.

Sense of Taste

Appeal to the taste came next in the study. Like the appeal to hearing, taste appeal fell almost exclusively into the categories of the "pleasant" and "unpleasant." The favorite taste of all was that of honey. Constantly, Spurgeon referred to it. One entire sermon topic centered around it: "Hands Full of Honey." Here are some examples of various taste appeals:

---

[5]Vol. 1, p. 95.
[6]Vol. 1, p. 123.
[7]Vol. 11, p. 201.
[8]Vol. 1, p. 279.
[9]Vol. 14, p. 324.

Suppose you tell me that honey is bitter. I reply, "No, I am sure you cannot have tasted it; taste it and try." [Note the direct appeal.] So it is with the Holy Ghost.[10]

In answering those who accused him of speaking bitterly he replied:

Very well; let it be so. Physic is often bitter, but it shall work well, and the physician is not bitter because the medicine is so.[11]

Elsewhere, he described the treatment of a text in terms of taste:

It is a text to be treated as the manna was that fell from heaven; namely, to be tasted, to be eaten, to be digested, and to be lived upon day to day.[12]

In contrast to what others say, the words of a friend, Spurgeon said, "are music; they taste like honey."[13] The drunkard received this warning:

I might picture thee, O drunkard, when thy cups are drained, and when thy liquor shall no longer be sweet to thy taste, when worse than gall shall be the dainties that thou drinkest.[14]

Here is a very apt taste description:

It does one good to see a hungry man eat his food. To him every bitter thing is sweet. He does not turn over his food and cut off every little bit of gristle, as some of you do because of your delicate appetites.[15]

Explaining Christian joy he exulted:

It is a joy which does not grow stale; you may keep it in your mouth by the year together, and yet it never cloys. . . . The world's gay folk are soon sick of their drink. . . . Christians have their sweets, and those are as honey and the honeycomb, the best of the best.[16]

---

[10]Vol. 1, p. 62.
[11]Vol. 8, p. 27.
[12]Vol. 10, p. 9.
[13]Vol. 1, p. 73. An interesting combination of Sound and Taste. It is almost as if he had said "the music is like honey."
[14]Vol. 1, p. 283.
[15]Vol. 19, p. 184.
[16]Vol. 14, p. 20.

One of Spurgeon's most graphic word-pictures, appealing to both sight and taste, was sketched in a sermon mentioned previously, "Hands Full of Honey." The Saviour is likened to Samson who has seized the honey from the carcass of the slain lion:

> With the honey in his hands, which he continues still to feast upon, he displays the heavenly sweetness to all that are round about him, saying, "O taste and see that the Lord is good: blessed is the man that trusteth in him."[17]

These quotations will have to suffice.

Sense of Smell

One sense remains: smell.

Again, the contrast between pleasant and unpleasant odors prevails; nothing more-or-less neutral nature was found.

Included here are some of his better passages, the first of which pertains to the burial of Christ: "It behooved him to slumber in the dust awhile, that he might perfume the chamber of the grave.[18] Perfume is one of his favorite figures:

> The precious perfume of the gospel must be poured forth to sweeten the air.[19]

> I have hope of a family when one child is converted; for grace is like precious ointment; it spreads a perfume all around. When a box of fragrant spice is put into a room, the perfume soon fills the entire chamber, then creeps silently up the stairs into the upper rooms, and ceases not its work until it has filled the whole house.[20]

> He puts our prayers, like rose leaves, between the pages of his book of remembrance, and when the volume is opened at last, there shall be a precious fragrance springing up therefrom.[21]

Seldom did he speak of foul odors, but when he did, it was almost always in contrast to some fragrant one. Here are two examples:

---

[17]Vol. 14, p. 11.
[18]Vol. 1, p. 67.
[19]Vol. 19, p. 323.
[20]Vol. 8, p. 86.
[21]Vol. 1, p. 173.

Does not unbelief, which is quite as obnoxious as brimstone, too often spoil the sweet odor of our supplications?[22]

The second is a beautiful means of teaching the fact of the non-corruptibility of the body of Christ during its death:

The vault is not damp with the vapors of death, nor doth the air contain ought of contagion. . . . In an ordinary tomb, "there are noxious smells of corruption. . . ."But in Christ's tomb, "there is no scent, yea, rather, a perfume."[23]

There can be but one conclusion from this evidence: the existence of Sense Appeal in the sermons of Spurgeon is noteworthy.[24] The evidence that I have amassed must be evaluated and principles deduced from it. But I shall not now do so. That must wait until a later chapter. It is enough to say here that Sense Appeal was a significant element in Spurgeon's preaching.

---

[22]C. H. Spurgeon, *Illustrations and Meditations*, p. 11. New York: Funk and Wagnalls, 1883.

[23]Vol. 1, p. 215.

[24]One factor which should impress contemporary preachers as noteworthy is Spurgeon's appeal to the whole man. In this day, when there is a renewed emphasis upon the unity of human nature, Spurgeon's appeal to all of the senses seems more up to date than much present preaching that is confined to eye appeal alone.

CHAPTER SIX
THE INFLUENCE OF SENSE APPEAL

Although the internal evidence in the previous chapters itself is conclusive, it will be well to note briefly how it is corroborated by external testimony. Others more-or-less unconsciously, have noted the same thing in less analytic fashion. Because they did not make a thorough study of the particular thesis of this book, their comments were naturally less specific in nature and more general in scope. However, that they "felt" the existence of Sense Appeal is indicated by statements that show awareness of it. But groping after an explanation of the influences that they *sensed* were being brought to bear upon them, they never quite grasped the precise nature of the strange, strong appealing quality.

Having pursued the thesis set forth in the preceding chapters, however, the reader is in a better position to appreciate and evaluate the writings of others and what was happening to them. He now can understand their feelings more clearly than they. He knows that one large factor in what they variously praised as "pungent, imaginative, rhetorically realistic" and the like, was what I have called Sense Appeal.

Apart from some statements by Blackwood (which are very definite about it), Brastow's remarks seem most discerning. He wrote of Spurgeon's sermons as "summoning men to the use of the same faculties in religion that they use in everyday life."[1] In "everyday life" all five senses are employed constantly. However, this advice has not normally been applied to preaching. In hearing a sermon, ordinarily one exercises only his senses of hearing and sight.[2] The other senses are rarely activated. Spurgeon, we have

---

[1]Brastow, *op. cit.,* p. 413.
[2]Both through word-appeal to the senses and merely in order to hear and see the speaker himself.

seen, caused the hearer to use all his senses. In fact, he demanded that they activate these through learning how to use their imaginations well. Brastow further observes:

> His statements of doctrine make more impression upon the imagination than upon the critical judgment. . . . He deals with Scripture in such a way that it catches the fancy, stirs an emotional interest. . . . He illustrates the value of a generous use of the imagination in deducing fruitful thought from the Scriptures.[3]

Brastow saw the importance of imagination. He referred to Spurgeon's use of "imagination" which in turn quickened the hearer's imagination, caught his fancy, and stirred his emotions. This is another way of saying that the listener "felt, saw, heard" etc., as though his senses had been stimulated by objective sense data. Brastow saw the subjective effect clearly, but vaguely attributed it to the usually ill-defined power of "imagination."[4] While it is true that Spurgeon's imaginative powers were stimulated, and the stirring of his hearer's imagination was the result, what means was used to convey this stirring from the one to the other? There can be but one answer: the use of a strong appeal to the senses.

Of course it was the Sense Appeal of objective stimuli (or memory of the same) that originally aroused Spurgeon's interest and activated his imagination. The only thing that could have possibly produced the same effect in his hearers' minds was a similar appeal. However, the further problem involved was the absence of objective stimuli to convey the sense expression in the preaching context. Therefore, evocative words had to replace objective stimuli. A successful substitution of words for objective visual, auditory, taste, kinesthetic and olfactory sensations demanded a disciplined art as true as that required to paint pictures on canvas. To paint word-pictures, describe sounds, tastes and odors, as well as touch sensations with such vividness and realism that one's hearers might

---

[3]*Op. cit.,* pp. 395,396,407.
[4]The precise meaning of this term and its relationship to other faculties involved in Sense Appeal is more fully discussed in a later chapter. While the word is used somewhat more loosely here, in accordance with broader concepts, its present use is still in accordance with the more precise one.

experience these sensations as though they were actually experiencing them objectively, demanded study and training even more rigorous than physical art. The latter employs objective data to represent the impression desired and is greatly aided thereby. But word description of color, shape, size, composition, action, etc. is far more difficult. That Spurgeon achieved this result is the unanimous testimony of those who heard him or read his sermons.

A. J. Gordon, for instance, writes, "Never shall I forget the passage in the sermon in which Mr. Spurgeon made us hear the angels harping with their harps."[5] Fernald describes the effect of one of Spurgeon's sermons upon him. He reports, Spurgeon exclaimed: "If Christ would come to that drunkard, and *wash his mouth out,* wouldn't that make Jesus Christ great?" He goes on to say, concerning the italicized words, "As he uttered them, they seemed to carry the entire physical and moral renovation of the man till you could see him cleansed from his pollution."[6] Note especially the words, "till you could see him cleansed." To their testimony, that of the writer of the introduction to the *Memorial Library* of Spurgeon's sermons must be added. He vividly and incisively states, "the eye *listens* scarcely less than the ear to the sweet-flowing oratory."[7] The following is recorded in the Greville Memoirs:

> He preached for about three-quarters of an hour, and to judge by the use of the handkerchiefs and the audible sobs, with great effect.[8]

All of these quotations attest to the strong impression that Sense Appeal made upon the hearers of Spurgeon's sermons. One speaks of practically "hearing" that which he describes; another of "seeing" a man cleansed; and a third, of the "eye listening" to Spurgeon's oratory. This last expression, graphic as it is, most clearly sets forth Sight Appeal. The eye listening, must be interpreted to mean that in listening to Spurgeon's vivid, realistic description, one virtually sees the scene described, so that he may be said to listen to the description

[5]Needham, *op. cit.,* pp. 4-5.
[6]In Pike's biography, *Memorial Library,* Vol. 20, p. 323.
[7]E. L. Magoon, Vol. 1, p.x.
[8]In Robert Shindler, *From the Usher's Desk to the Tabernacle Pulpit,* p. 102. New York: A. C. Armstrong and Son, 1893.

as much with the eye as with the ear. He hears not mere words alone, but as he listens what he hears enables him to "see" what the preacher depicts. It was no wonder that "audible sobs" were heard. Perhaps such sobs arose as Spurgeon pictured the following scene of one suffering in hell:

> See how his tongue hangs from between his blistered lips; how it excoriates and burns the roof of his mouth as if it were a firebrand. Behold him crying for a drop of water. I will not picture the scene. . . . O sinner! Lift thine eyes and behold the frowning countenance of God, for he is angry with you.[9]

Nothing short of the most effective rapport in Sense Appeal, in which the hearers were made to "see, hear" and "touch" as though they objectively did so, could draw tears and sobs from a congregation. Undoubtedly, it was passages such as the one just quoted that produced this effect.

H. G. Weston speaks of the transmission of Spurgeon's own sense perception to the hearer:

> He easily conveys to others his own sense of the depth and richness of the truth, and never toils, as so many, with effort to impart his feeling to his hearers.[10]

The Temple Bar magazine wrote,

> When he has concluded a sermon with a burst of his truly inspired eloquence, "he leaves" the whole of his congregation amazed, and the vast majority of its members anxious or hopeful, but in any case roused as if they had seen the heavens open.[11]

The last quotation is interesting, because it emphasizes that no matter what the varying reactions of the different members of the congregation might have been, one thing all were sure to experience

---

[9]Vol. 1, p. 189.
[10]Wayland, *op. cit.,* p. 75.
[11]*Ibid.,* p. 93.

was a quickening of their senses so as to "see" the spiritual pictures that he painted of heaven. The *Speaker* characterized him as a preacher,

> whose bright, simple, picturesque, and always forcible utterances were pitched in a key which attuned itself to every ear, and found entrance in every heart.[12]

J. H. Rushbrooke described his style this way: "He introduced a new note of realism into the pulpit."[13] Undoubtedly, Sense Appeal was the chief factor in producing this "realism." Edwin C. Dargan speaks of him in terms of observation and imagination (which are a part of Sense Appeal):

> In intellect he was alert, clever, sound, and strong, with fine imagination, large and shrewd observation, and wide reading, with retentive memory.[14]

Such personal testimony from the pens of capable and impartial critics (some of whom were professors of homiletics) cannot be set aside lightly.[15] It affords unmistakable evidence of the existence of Sense Appeal from a practical context. Whereas in the previous chapters, overwhelming proof was given of the existence of Sense Appeal from a study of the sermons themselves, this chapter has brought forth witnesses to the effects (and effectiveness) of this appeal upon the hearer. The significance of Sense Appeal in the preaching of Charles Haddon Spurgeon, therefore, has been demonstrated from the analytical and practical viewpoints; from the internal and external evidence. Why, do you think it is that the average modern day congregation is so unaffected and undemonstrative? Could it be—at least in part—because contemporary preachers by dull, lifeless, abstract preaching fail to appeal to their senses?

---

[12]*Ibid.,* p. 288.
[13]*A History of the English Baptists,* p. 219. London: The Baptist Publication Dept., 1947.
[14]*A History of Preaching,* Vol. 1, 538. Grand Rapids: Baker Book House, 1954.
[15]Especially since these quotations are all passing comments. None of these men was discussing Sense Appeal as such. And yet, each of them mentions factors that, it will be shown, are essential elements of Sense Appeal.

CHAPTER SEVEN
THE ORIGIN OF SPURGEON'S SENSE APPEAL

The influence of Spurgeon's conversion was mentioned as a significant factor in the origin of Sense Appeal. This influence was significant, but not the sole factor to be considered. Something too was said of the role that his early home life played in its development.[1] How important were these and other acquired factors? Was his ability to appeal to the senses mostly innate or mainly acquired? The value of determining this is apparent. If conveying Sense Appeal is wholly (or even mostly) an inherited ability, it is useless to study the subject further, so far as all practical purposes are concerned, for those devoid of such natural qualities would find nothing but discouragement in its pursuit.

It is a simple matter to multiply quotations attesting to Spurgeon's exceptional *natural abilities*. Yet, these judgments are wholly unsupported by facts. That they come from faulty assumptions I shall try to show. Two typical samples follow: "He was a student by nature."[2] How does the writer know this? Is it not just as possible that these studious interests (which admittedly were active at an early age) may have been stimulated and encouraged largely by the intellectual atmosphere of his grandfather's home?[3] Brastow claims, "Mr. Spurgeon was a man of extraordinary native

---

[1]Chapter One F. R. Webber's statement, tying the beginning of his reading interests to his conversion, may be added. He reports that immediately following his conversion, "Spurgeon began to read with increased interest the Bible, and the books of the Puritan writers, which he found in his grandfather's library." *A History of Preaching,* Vol. 1, p. 596. Milwaukee: Northwestern Publishing House, 1952.

[2]Lorimer, *op. cit.,* p. 71.

[3]Magoon implies as much: "He accumulated no small amount of literary treasure; but his best acquisitions were secured in the early and accurate knowledge of human nature, which, through juvenile discipline in diversified life, Providence caused him to possess." *Op. cit.,* p. vii.

preaching gifts."[4] But, again, he offers no proofs. Such an important question cannot be answered merely by affirmations. That Spurgeon had exceptional gifts is conceded. But that he possessed "extraordinary native *preaching* gifts" would be extraordinary indeed! Moreover, *gifts,* according to the New Testament, must be developed. One wonders whether Brastow himself could have defined a *"native* preaching gift." Moreover, it should be observed, this unsupported claim is in direct conflict with considerable evidence (as you will see) that indicates that his preaching abilities largely were developed from hard work.

While judging no one's motives, it is important to point out that there is a sinful tendency within every individual to devaluate the efforts of another, especially when he is a contemporary in the same field who far excels him. How easy it is to avoid the unpleasant implications of another's success wrought mainly through labor and hard work by attributing it to his "native abilities."[5] If it were acquired, the reviewer also might have acquired it; that he did not, casts some reflection upon him. Therefore, it is a relief to rationalize their success away by asserting that the ability of all great men is due to inherited factors.

Garvie's better-balanced judgment seems a bit more objective. Yet it still falls short of the mark. What he wrote of language was true about other aspects of Spurgeon's preaching and about Sense Appeal in particular:

> Not only was such racy English native to this genius; his early training and surroundings have been favorable to this gift, and he afterwards cultivated it by close study of the masters of the language.[6]

This statement marks out three sources, two acquired and one innate. To these three (his talent or natural abilities, early training

---

[4]*Op. cit.,* p. 401.

[5]Broadus rightly notes: "Power of description is of course partly a natural gift; but many intelligent men will marvel and lament that they cannot describe, when they have never fairly tried—never given themselves any general training in that respect, nor ever really studied any one scene or object which they attempted to describe." *Op. cit.,* p. 160.

[6]Alfred E. Garvie, *The Christian Preacher,* p. 249. New York: Charles Scribner's Sons, 1921. "Racy English," however, is never inherited, but always acquired.

and environment and subsequent laborious study) personal experience should be added as a fourth and final source.

There is sufficient testimony on the part of Spurgeon himself to prove that hard work and conscious study of preaching techniques made a large contribution. He *worked* to produce sermons "shaped to attract men."[7] In his *Lectures* to his students, Spurgeon revealed much of his own method of sermon preparation. Everywhere, self-conscious effort to analyze and improve preaching is evident. He showed awareness of the need to employ special techniques in order to keep "out of the rut of dull formality."[8] With him, sermons had to be built, piece by piece. He analyzed introductions and advised, "the introduction should have something striking in it."[9] He thought illustrations so important, that he devoted an entire volume to their consideration. The summary of what he said there throws light both upon his art of illustration and the conscious effort he made to perceive those things about him that he might use to teach God's truth with clarity. No one reading the following passage should fail to see that a well developed perception, according to Spurgeon, was not so much a matter of one's innate ability as the result of regular effort to discover raw materials in nature that he might manufacture into sermons:

> Keep your eyes open, and gather flowers from the garden and field with your own hands; they will be far more acceptable than withered specimens borrowed from other men's bouquets, however beautiful those may once have been.[10]

Other passages further disclose this process of acquisition of materials from the sense realm:

> Can you not learn from nature? Every flower is waiting to teach you. "Consider the lilies," and learn from the roses. . . . There is a voice in every gale, and a lesson in every grain of dust it bears. Sermons glisten in the morning on every blade of grass, and homilies fly by as the sere leaves fall from the trees. A forest is a library, a corn-field is a volume of philosophy, the rock is a

---

[7]Gordon in Needham, *op. cit.*, p. viii.
[8]C. H. Spurgeon, *Lectures to my Students*, p. 157. New York: American Tract Society, n.d.
[9]*Ibid.*, p. 216.
[10]*Lectures*, p. 221.

history, and the river at its base a poem. . . . Books are poor things compared with these.[11]

He further recommends:

In your sermons cultivate what Father Taylor calls "the surprise power. . . ." Do not say what everybody expected you to say. . . . Let your thunderbolt drop out of a clear sky.[12]

This last quotation shows not only thoughtful, deliberate technique, but also previous study of technique in the writings of others.[13] And, perhaps of greatest importance is the fact that through books and in lectures at his pastor's college, Spurgeon attempted to teach others how to preach. Evidently, it was his view that the methods of preaching in which he believed were communicable to any man of basic ability and gifts, and that such a man could by prayerful diligence acquire them.

As to the use of language and voice, he criticized the preaching of those whose "tame phrases, hackneyed expressions, and dreary monotones make the staple of their discourses."[14] Spurgeon tells us that he acquired not only technique, but even the very wording of others. He declared, "The collection of a fund of ideas *and expressions* is exceedingly helpful."[15] And quite contrary to those who attribute his vocabulary, style, or language to native ability, he maintained,

Second only to a store of ideas is a rich vocabulary. Beauties of language, elegancies of speech, and above all forcible sentences are to be selected, remembered, and imitated.[16]

---

[11]*Ibid.*, p. 293.

[12]*Ibid.*, pp. 222-223.

[13]Spurgeon's debt to the Puritan writers is freely confessed. He said, "I have preached them all." Brastow, *op. cit.*, p. 389. But, it is important to note that he did so with discernment. He never preached them word for word, thought for thought uncritically as some do now. Rather, he distilled the best from them, threw away what he disagreed with, and cast all into the new mould of his own presentation.

[14]*Lectures*, p. 223.

[15]*Ibid.*, p. 236.

[16]*Ibid.*, p. 237. This clearly modifies such unqualified and misleading statements as this one by Ilion T. Jones: "Spurgeon said he never composed a sentence in advance." If they were not composed on paper, they were often composed in the mind. *Principles and Practice of Preaching*, p. 188. New York: Abingdon Press, 1956.

And with respect to the labor required in obtaining fruitful ideas he entertained no doubts:

> There is much virtue which is like the juice of the grape, which has to be squeezed before you get it; not like the generous drop of the honeycomb, distilling willingly and freely.[17]

The idea that, like Minerva, springing from the head of Zeus fully armed, Spurgeon came into this world with natural ability for preaching, hardly coincides with the evidence already presented. Another statement by Brastow far more accurately sizes up the facts:

> His sermons in his early years are full of illustrations wrought up from his reading. . . . He observed the thought, appropriated the method, as he caught the style of the old Puritan preachers.[18]

He further wrote:

> One notes readily, also, that his mind is completely saturated with Biblical diction. . . . His rhetoric has been nurtured from. . . Christian hymns, and especially the old Puritan writers. They impart a graceful, rhythmic movement to his sentences. . . . One fancies that his use of figurative language, in which the metaphor, apostrophe, and interrogation abound. . . was the result. . . of his familiarity with the language of the Bible.[19]

It seems clear, then, that Spurgeon is no exception to this important generalization: "At some early stage almost every master preacher has made a study of printed sermons by former divines."[20] E. L. Magoon summarizes the facts concerning Spurgeon:

> He has rare powers of observation, recollection, assimilation, and creation. . . . He seems to have opened his eyes to nature in all its varieties; to science in all its discoveries, and to literature in all its departments. Everything which the eye of man can look

---

[17]Magoon, *op. cit.*, p. viii.
[18]*Op. cit.*, p. 391.
[19]*Ibid.*, p. 410.
[20]A. W. Blackwood, Editor, *The Protestant Pulpit*, p. 5. New York: Nashville: Abingdon Press, 1947.

upon, or the ear hear, seems to have made an indelible impression on his mental powers. . . . Out of the forms of beauty which his eyes see, other still lovelier forms are created. The loveliest natural landscape is adorned with additional beauty, by the aid of a refined and chastened fancy. . . . These higher qualities are evidently aided by a close study of the graces of speaking. The natural has been aided by study,—the gifts of the orator by the graces.[21]

Spurgeon did have remarkable innate qualities. No one wishes to deny that fact. But these would have been worthless apart from the intense and untiring efforts he expended to develop them for preaching. They were disciplined, enlarged, and supplemented by acquisitions from the best past literature. Preaching was analyzed, discussed and formulated into working principles and techniques in a conscious theory of preaching. Spurgeon was almost wholly caught up in preaching. He thought about it, taught it, discussed it and continually worked at it. Natural ability views ignore these facts.

What may be said, then, of the value of studying Spurgeon's sermons? Is it a worthwhile enterprise? Or, is it profitable only to those who are born with extraordinary powers?

The value of such sermon study readily may be seen from the evidence in this chapter. It is certain that a large part of Spurgeon's preaching ability was acquired and not innate. Within all who are called to the ministry there is some innate ability. For those with less natural ability than Spurgeon there is not less, but even more necessity for study. If Spurgeon's larger abilities required the discipline and development that can be gained only through such study, surely those of lesser natural powers require it too. Where is a better place to begin than with Spurgeon? With what aspect of his preaching might one better begin his study than with Sense Appeal in this day in which right brain learning is so well-developed?

It is probably true that since Spurgeon had more than average natural ability, others may not expect to become Spurgeons. But, the lesson taught by the fact of Spurgeon's success is that whatever

---

[21]*Op. cit.*, p. xi.

natural ability one possesses, it still demands the utmost training, refining, and supplementary study. With proper training one is able to rise far above capabilities resulting from innate ability alone. Sense Appeal, therefore, must be studied strictly from the viewpoint of *acquired* technique and methodology, as it has been here.

I wish to open a second question and to discuss it briefly. Is progress and refinement in technique evident in Spurgeon's sermons? On this question, the reviewers are divided. Some maintain that there was retrogression rather than progress. They see more vitality and spontaneity in the earlier sermons. One author writes, "I am inclined to think that Mr. Spurgeon gave a little more play to the imagination then than now."[22] Another writes:

> His eloquence was more fervid and impetuous than it became as years passed on. But it was also more original, more imaginative, more inspiring. Much has changed in the great preacher since then. He has become what he was not in those days, but what he most undoubtedly is now, a great man.[23]

The sermons in the *Memorial Library* do reveal a decline in the *quantity* of Sense Appeal. But they also exhibit a tendency toward finer *quality*. Lorimer says, in confirmation of this:

> At the beginning of his ministry he may have allowed his imagination a fuller range than was best, and may have found it difficult to restrain a tendency toward odd turns of thought and homey illustrations.[24]

After criticizing several noticeable defects that were apparent in Spurgeon's earlier sermons, the author of *Representative Modern Preachers* writes, "These faults he measurably overcame in his later ministry."[25] Spurgeon, looking back to his early preaching, said, "Once, I put all my knowledge together in glorious confusion, but now I have a shelf in my head for everything.[26]

It is impossible to believe that one who studied and worked at the improvement of preaching so laboriously could have failed to

[22]Needham, *op. cit.,* p. 5.
[23]T. H. Pattison, in Wayland, *op. cit.,* p. 92.
[24]*Op. cit.,* p. 33.
[25]*Op. cit.,* p. 406.
[26]Shindler, *op. cit.,* p. 88.

improve his style. Lorimer paints a picture of his never-failing zeal for improvement:

> He assiduously added to his originally scant acquaintance with the dead languages, and unquestionally neglected not the French; and was more familiar with theological literature, especially with Puritan writings, than two-thirds of our more pretentious erudite teachers and preachers. He knew so much that it was unnecessary for him to make a parade of his knowledge. . . . As Joseph Cook has said, he had in perfection, the art of keeping the reservoir well supplied.[27]

And Brown categorically affirms such growth:

> It is to be noted that the power (of speech) grew—grew by deepening acquaintance with the writings of men conspicuous for the strength and grandeur of their English style. . . .[28]

It must be remembered, too, that age tempers. It usually tends to make one more conservative. And, in addition, Spurgeon's physical maladies undoubtedly took their toll throughout the years, sapping something of his early strength and vitality from him. W. E. Hatcher, who knew and worked intimately with him, describes the severity of these illnesses (noting especially how the difficulties became intensified in later years). Especially severe was his bout with gout:

> Mr. Spurgeon worked all the time under weights. It is doubtful whether he had one moment of absolute freedom from pain for years of his later life.

> Rheumatic gout was the supreme affliction of his life. I suppose it grew worse and worse. . . . He said that he suffered sorely from the swellings of his feet and hands. Upon leaving the bed in the mornings he would have much difficulty in using his feet. They would be much swollen and acutely sensitive to touch, and he had to rub and use them by degrees until he could stand upon them. As a fact his gait was slow and unsteady, and not infrequently he had falls that were painful and dangerous.

[27]*Op. cit.*, pp. 71-72.
[28]*Op. cit.*, p. 226.

Often when he waked in the morning, his right hand was as rigidly locked as if it had been petrified. Not a joint could be unbent by the force of its own muscles. He had to take it finger by finger, and joint by joint, and so work and loosen its machinery as to restore it to action.[29]

It would seem correct to say that although the quantity and intensity of Sense Appeal abated, the quality mounted. Suffering, as well as age, mellowed it, while study enhanced and refined it.

While enough has been said with respect to Spurgeon's dependence upon the writings of others in general, and something more specific concerning the importance of the Puritans, it is necessary to note briefly the great contribution of one writer in particular. "Old John Bunyan," as Spurgeon often affectionately called him, more than any other person influenced his preaching. In Spurgeon's sermons, he is the most quoted of all writers. His influence can be traced everywhere. No volume fails to carry his name; often it is echoed successively in sermon after sermon.

For our present purposes, it is important to notice that *above all else* Bunyan's highly descriptive allegorical style stresses Sense Appeal. One entire book, *The Holy War,*[30] is based upon the invasion of "Mansoul" *by means of his senses.* Probably no writer in history so mastered the art of Sense Appeal as he. And, note, Bunyan was Spurgeon's avowed favorite. From a child, he read, reread, digested and synthesized much from his writings. He does not hesitate to declare:

> Next to the Bible, the book that I value most is John Bunyan's "Pilgrim's Progress," and I imagine that I may have read that through perhaps a hundred times. It is a book of which I never seem to tire.[31]

---

[29]Wayland, *op. cit.,* pp. 187-188.

[30]Spurgeon refers specifically to this book in Vol. 6, pp. 224-225.

[31]Bunyan says, "This miry slough is such a place as cannot be mended," but Spurgeon undertakes to do so with Scripture promises! He would perhaps agree with Bunyan that Millions of "cart-loads. . . of wholesome instructions" could not do the job. But in the promises of God, he finds the proper "materials" to "mend" the place.

All of Bunyan's books are quoted, cited or expanded. They form a never-failing source for sermon ideas. His own vocabulary, and his thought-forms were partly molded by them. Take, for example, the following quotation that appeared in a sermon that makes no reference to Bunyan at all. It is clearly reminiscent of Bunyan's "Slough of Despond," but possibly unconsciously so: "It should be our endeavour to cast loads of promises into every slough that runs across the path." While the basic imagery was Bunyan's, Spurgeon's use of it shows an advance. It was not unsynthesized, but digested, combined with other concepts, and then used so that the further thought of filling in those sloughs with Scripture promises was offered. It is wrong, therefore, to suggest that Spurgeon was a carbon copy of Bunyan.

Several biographers draw some connection between the two men, but without sufficient emphasis. Brastow, although styling Spurgeon "The Puritan Pastoral Evangelist," makes no mention of Bunyan whatever. Needham merely notes his youthful interest in the latter's writings:

> He would sit for hours together gazing with childish horror at the grim figures of "Old Bonner" and "Giant Despair"; or tracing the adventures of Christian in the "Pilgrim's Progress."[32]

And Wayland seems satisfied in saying, "He used the English of Bunyan and of Abraham Lincoln."[33] The English of Bunyan—a hearty "yes." But the English of Lincoln—? However, Wayland does include a valuable excerpt from the diary of J. D. Everett, containing his impressions of Spurgeon at the age of fifteen. Everett wrote, "I have also heard him recite long passages from Bunyan's 'Grace Abounding.'"[34] This indicates that Spurgeon had an early, intimate acquaintance with his works. Finally, Lorimer writes (with more insight than the rest): "Spurgeon approached nearer to Bunyan than any other in the quality of his imagination."[35] He

---

[32]*Op. cit.*, p. 29.
[33]*Op. cit.*, p. 38.
[34]*Ibid.*, p. 14.
[35]*Op. cit.*, p. 11.

recognizes that the crucial point of contact between the two lies in the realm of Sense Appeal (which he calls imagination). It would be of interest to pursue this relationship further, but to do justice to this matter would require another study as long as the present one. This much, then, must suffice.

It seems conclusive from the evidence adduced in this chapter, that Spurgeon, though a man endowed with many hereditary gifts, largely owed his success to the efforts he expended in the diligent study of the writings of others. But why has this not been seen before? I have suggested earlier one reason: human perversity (it makes the rest of us look bad). But there is at least another. One reason why so much has been attributed to nature rather than nurture, is that a misinterpretation of the fact of Spurgeon's youthful success prevails. It is commonly supposed that since his preaching was good from the earliest sermons on, this manifest ability to preach must have been the result of native gifts. However, we have seen that Spurgeon attributed his results to God's blessings upon the hard work and study that he did. Can these two facts be harmonized? Easily; much study was done at an extremely early age. This is the point that seems to have been forgotten. Unlike most of us, from earliest youth onward he was trained (and learned to train himself) in the very things that later were to make him a master preacher.[36] Throughout his later ministry, he was able to classify, refurbish and supplement the early studies which stood him in such good stead for life.

To those who would follow in his steps, this truth must be emphasized: there is no short cut to good preaching. Study, time, and hard work are the only means whereby the techniques of Sense Appeal may be acquired. Fortunately, the study sources are still the same as those available to Spurgeon—with one important exception: there is now available much more literature to which Spurgeon did not have access, and one magnificent source in particular—Spurgeon's sermons themselves! As Spurgeon studied Bunyan's works, so today, one may profitably study Spurgeon's.

---

[36]Shindler writes, "From another person. . . we gather that his early addresses were very instructive, often including illustrations derived from history, geography, astronomy, and other branches of science." *Op. cit.,* p. 52. Such illustrative materials cannot be inherited, but only acquired by study. That his first sermons contained them in abundance, is a clear proof of this early intensive study. His library (now in William Jewell College, Liberty, Missouri), contains nearly as many scientific books as theological and religious ones.

CHAPTER EIGHT
THE ELEMENTS OF SENSE APPEAL

Spurgeon's development of the techniques of Sense Appeal involved an orderly process. And, encouragingly enough, there is nothing mysterious about it. The appeal was dependent upon certain identifiable factors as surely as was the original activation of his senses dependent upon objective stimuli. Three factors, when properly combined, produce Sense Appeal: Perception, Imagination,[1] and Description.

The first of these represents the ability to apprehend the sense realm itself; the second, the synthesizing ability to relate sense data to revealed truth in order to illuminate the latter; the third, the ability to describe the above to others (by means of words alone[2]) with such vividness that they too, might experience the same sense impression and the same synthesis with Divine truth as the speaker.

The law of Sense Appeal may be expressed as a mathematical formula: Sense Perception, plus Synthetic Imagination, plus Realistic Description equals Sense Appeal.

It is helpful to look upon the three factors in terms of the manufacture of goods. Sense Perception may be equated with the obtaining of raw materials, Synthetic Imagination with the refining of the same in the manufacture of the product, and Realistic Description with the strategies, policies and means of distribution. In Spurgeon there was a happy and harmonious combination of the

---

[1]The use of the word "imagination" here is narrower than that of Blackwood, corresponding to the latter half of his definition, namely, "the ability. . . to put things together." The former half he separately designated, "Perception." Cf., *The Protestant Pulpit, op. cit.,* p. 306.

[2]Of course, this does not exclude voice and gesture, which are important elements in Description proper, but fall outside the scope of this book.

three, each of which was developed to a high and equal degree. Often, in other preachers one or more is undeveloped. But, like the proverbial "weak link" in a chain, defection in any one (even though, the other two be strong) renders the others ineffective, and consequently destroys the effectiveness of Sense Appeal. Without a keen sense of Perception, Sense Appeal suffers from a lack of raw material. Under such conditions the machinery of Synthetic Imagination soon rusts from disuse and descriptive powers never get much opportunity for development. Harrington and Fulton say:

> If one would tell a story clearly, vividly, thrillingly, he must himself see clearly and feel keenly the pictures and impressions of life he is trying to present to others.[3]

The same is just as true concerning Sense Appeal.

If Synthetic Imagination is weak, raw materials unrefined and unrelated to truth will be conveyed in a rough, illogical and unappealing form. And when the power of Realistic Description is underdeveloped, even the keenest Perception, combined in the finest synthesis with truth is worthless, because faulty description will bottle up the flow of the best product. Therefore, each element of Sense Appeal must be considered important in itself and essential in its relationships to the other two. No one of them may be over-emphasized or minimized.[4]

Before the proper function and relationships of each may be demonstrated by means of a concrete example, one further observation must be made. Spurgeon had only words with which to work. The extreme difficulty of word craftmanship may be further discerned from the fact that these words had to be so fashioned that they would quicken the imagination by way of the memory. Memory contains the experience of various sense perceptions stored away. But it possesses nothing not previously experienced. Spurgeon, therefore, had to know what experiences were common to his hearers. Then he had to frame his appeal with clarity,

---

[3]W. L. Harrington, M. G. Fulton, *Talking Well*, p. 27. New York: The Macmillan Co., 1925.

[4]John Brown well described the process when he wrote of Spurgeon's "mind readily taking in all he saw and heard and read, and giving it out again with fullness and freshness." *Op. cit.*, p. 223. "Taking in" = Perception, "Giving out" = Description and "freshness" = Imagination.

simplicity and interest (a difficult combination indeed) not only to awaken memory but also to arouse vital interest. Ivory tower sermons do not do this. He had to live and move among his people, and think about the best ways to reach them with the Word. This involved effort and struggle. Listen to him searching for some smouldering ember of sense perception buried deep in the memory of every hearer; observe him as he discovers and rekindles it into a burning fire:

> Go back man; sing of that moment, and then thou wilt have a song in the night. Or if thou hast almost forgotten that, then sure thou hast some precious milestone along the road of life that is not quite grown over with moss, on which thou canst read some happy inscription of His mercy toward thee![5]

In describing new things (i.e., those which the hearer has never experienced) there is no memory through which to reach the imagination. The same is true of spiritual things (of which there is no sense perception). Such appeal had to be made by means of comparison with and analogy to the known. Brastow observes: "He appeals. . . to men's common interests and experiences, to their feelings, predispositions and interests."[6] But it is impossible to describe something totally unlike everything else.[7] But he believed that all created things, whether material or spiritual, have likenesses to one another, since they were made by the same Hand. Truths of the spiritual realm, moreover, for the same reason may be likened not only to those within that realm, but to things within the material realm.[8] Of making such comparisons, Spurgeon was a master. Take,

---

[5]*The Protestant Pulpit, op. cit.*, p. 119.
[6]*Op. cit.*, p. 119.
[7]Spurgeon was aware of this impossibility, as even his acute powers of description were exhausted in an attempt to describe Christ. He says, "In vain does the minister dilate upon his charms; in vain does he try to paint his features as well as he can. We are poor daubers, and we mar the beauty which we attempt to portray." Vol. 4, p. 103.
[8]Spurgeon said, "That which can be seen, tasted, and touched, and handled is meant to be to us the outward and visible sign of a something which we find in the Word of God, and in our spiritual experience." *The Art of Illustration*, p. 123. He insisted this was the prophets' method: "They. . . described what they saw with spiritual eyes after the form or fashion of something which could be seen by the eye of nature." Vol. 6, p. 216.

for instance, his description of the lasting quality of Christian joy in contrast to the world's ephemeral mirth:

> But the Christian's delight is like a steady coal fire. You have seen the grate full of coals all burning red, and the whole mass of coal has seemed to be one great glowing ruby and everybody who has come into the room out of the cold has delighted to warm his hands for it gives out a steady heat and warms the body even to its marrow. Such are our joys.[9]

Christian joy is intangible. It is, therefore, difficult to describe to one who has never known it. Its lasting quality in contrast to passing pleasures was the major point. So Spurgeon likened it to an experience that was common to every one of his hearers in a day when heating was primarily achieved by means of the open hearth. The comparison was expertly made. Not only did he illustrate his point (the unknown by means of the known) but did so by means of an analogy entirely compatible with joy. He might have used water for the comparison, illustrating how freezing solidifies an unstable element. Inexpert preachers do this all of the time. But the analogy would suffer because of secondary factors. The incompatibility of Christian joy (which has decidedly "warm" connotations) and ice is apparent. It was a master's hand, therefore, that selected the coal fire.

The principal factors involved in Sense Appeal have been set forth. But how did these function in a specific situation? It will be well to trace an actual instance throughout the process outlined above.

The following passage, from a sermon entitled, "A View of God's Glory" (a *title* with Sense Appeal) is a good example:

> Consider the goodness of God in creation. Who could ever tell all God's goodness there? Why, every creek that runs up into the shore is full of it where the fry dance in the water. Why, every tree and every forest rings with it; where feathered songsters sit and make their wings quiver with delight and ecstacy. Why every atom of this air, which is dense with animalculae, is full of God's goodness. The cattle on a thousand hills he feeds; the

---

[9]Vol. 14, pp. 19-20.

ravens come and peck their food from his liberal hands. The fishes leap out of their element, and he supplies them; every insect is nourished by him. The lion roars in the forest for his prey, and he sendeth it to him. Ten thousand creatures are all fed by him.[10]

Analysis shows the paragraph contains everything previously noted. First, there is both direct and indirect appeal. Directly, Spurgeon addressed the hearer, calling upon him to "Consider" what he has to say. Then, indirectly, he appealed to the sense of sight and hearing. Before the mind pass mental images (drawn from past memories) of woodland and farmyard scenes, as he sketches them one by one. Birds sing, and the rustle of their wings is heard; cattle pepper the hills and insects buzz through the air. The sermon is alive with reality!

Sense Perception

Notice that there is a keen sense of Perception behind these words. They were not conceived wholly in the study; they could not be. This sort of preaching is the fruit of actual observation by one who had tramped through the woods.[11] He had stood by the creek and watched the schools of newly spawned minnows glittering in the sun. The flash of their rhythmic movements reminded him of a dance. Not only had he listened to the song of the bird, as he walked along, but he had stopped to watch and conjecture as to the meaning of its movements. Who can doubt that he had often visited a nearby pond (perhaps to fish) at daybreak or dusk and watched the bass breaking water to catch a bug when he says, "The fishes leap out of their element, and he supplies them?" He had, without a doubt, what Blackwood calls, "a lively imagination at work among facts of life."[12]

---

[10]Vol. 2, p. 208.

[11]Lorimer, op. cit., pp. 22-23, says, "Mr. Spurgeon was born in Kelvedon, Essex" (which he describes as a "rural retreat"). He continues, "The little boy. . . loved nature and never did his heart wander from his first love. He never could endure a stiffling atmosphere; his eyes continually hungered for the sight of green fields; and his homestead in later years was always so situated that his ears could drink in the song of the morning lark and the matin strains of the nightingale, and his heart feel the sweet and refining influence that comes from wood and vale."

[12]A. W. Blackwood, Biographical Preaching for Today, p. 140. New York: Abingdon Press, 1954.

When he beckoned to the air around him and spoke of the density of "animalculae" filling it, he revealed something of his knowledge of contemporary biology. Other passages indicate an intimate familiarity with all of the major sciences of the day.[13] Thus, he was not only a man of nature, but a man of the book as well. Consider the hours of astronomical study behind the following quotation:

> I might style Isaiah the pole-star of prophecy; Jeremiah resembles the rainy Hyades of Horace; Ezekiel was the burning Sirius; and as for Daniel, he resembles a flaming comet, flashing on our vision but for a moment, and then lost in obscurity. I am not at a loss to find a constellation for the minor prophets; they are a sweet group, of intense brilliancy, even though but small: they are the Pleiades of the Bible.[14]

W. R. Nicholl was correct when he stated, "Mr. Spurgeon's almost supernatural keenness of observation was a great element of his eloquence."[15] And Magoon did not overstate the facts when he declared:

> He has rare powers of observation. . . . His field of observation is wide and varied. He seems to have opened his eyes to *nature* in all its varieties; to science in all its discoveries, and to *literature* in all its departments. Everything which the eye of man can look upon, or the ear hear, seems to have made an indelible impression on his mental powers.[16]

Spurgeon himself had a great deal to say about Sense Perception. He holds Christ forth as the perfect example ot it. Pointedly, he maintains that He spoke, "as never man spake before, and yet as any observant man should speak."[17] All creation was a vast source of raw materials for Spurgeon. He believed it could become such for every preacher. Therefore, he said, "Opening our eyes, we shall

[13]Brastow says, "With works on geography, history, biography, poetry, and general popular literature he was at home." *Op. cit.,* p. 389.

[14]Vol. 2, p. 220.

[15]*Princes of the Church,* p. 48. London: Hodder and Stoughton, 1921. However, it is important to remember that this "keenness of observation" was mostly acquired, and neither supernatural nor even natural.

[16]*Op. cit.,* p. x.

[17]*The Art of Illustration, op. cit.,* p. 25.

discover abundant imagery all around."[18] One of his impressive uses of sight appeal is found in a passage in which Spurgeon strongly urges its use:

> The whole world is hung round by God with pictures; and the preacher has only to take them down, one by one, and hold them up before his congregation. . . . But he must have his own eyes open or he will not see these pictures.[19]

In short, he was able to appeal to others, because he "was impelled by something acutely felt."[20]

Synthetic Imagination

But more than Perception was needed to produce the sermon paragraph under consideration. The next obvious factor was Spurgeon's Synthesizing Imagination. Perhaps Brastow has best described this synthetic ability as well as noted its origin. He observes:

> He has the skill of the old Puritan preachers in repeating his text, or parts of it, in a great variety of connections throughout the sermon so as to keep it constantly before the mind, bringing it into relation with a great variety of thoughts, thus throwing new light upon it, and making it the more impressive.[21]

This synthetic Imagination was more than mere ornamentation or illustration. R. W. Dale has distinguished between such amateurish imitation and true synthetic ability. He characterized the former as "dressing. . . thoughts in imagery," and the latter as "incarnating"[22] them. He speaks derogatorily of sermons "overlaid with ornament," and declares:

> Mere ornament, instead of making our meaning clearer, is likely to conceal it, just as architectural decoration sometimes

---

[18]*Ibid.*, p. 25.
[19]*Ibid.*, p. 126.
[20]Magoon, *The Modern Whitfield*, p. v. New York: Sheldon, Blakeman and Co., 1856.
[21]*Op. cit.*, p. 410.
[22]*Nine Lectures on Preaching*, p. 46. New York: Hodder and Stoughton, n.d. Lorimer uses similar language when he writes of Spurgeon's "embodiment" of "ideas. . . in metaphor or figure that arrests thought by charming the imagination." This ability, he also says, "invests ideas with a living force." *Op. cit.*, p. 73.

conceals the true lines of a building. It is not of ornament I am thinking, but of firm and vigorous expression of our thoughts.[23]

And Spurgeon himself declared, "Our figures are meant not so much to be seen as seen through."[24]

Who but one with such Synthetic Imagination would have blended clouds of invisible bacteria with the goodness of God? But stressing the fact that God feeds and cares for each of these as individually as the lion in the forest, in a fresh and interesting way enlarges one's conception of the infinite goodness of God in creation.

Perhaps the astronomical quotation even more clearly demonstrates the necessity and role of Synthetic Imagination. To bring together the minor prophets and the constellation of Pleiades, required awareness of the possibilities of aligning all of physical reality with spiritual truths. Some study the stars as an end in themselves, and therefore, do not know how to connect their study with Christian teaching. Spiritual truths remain isolated entities unsynthesized (or as Dale would say, "unincarnated") with sense activating facts. Synthetic Imagination, on the other hand, takes the same truths and vividly, impressively, and appealingly merges them with Sense Experience. Blackwood writes of the interplay between Perception and Imagination:

> Spurgeon formed the habit of finding in unexpected places the germ-thoughts of future messages. He saw ships and preached from the passage "There go the ships." What he made out of that subject depended on the way his imagination kept working.[25]

Spurgeon is a good example of the extent to which one's imagination may be awakened. He said,

> I know my imagination sometimes has been so powerful that I could almost, when I have been alone at night, fancy I saw an

---

[23]Dale, *op. cit.,* pp. 44-57.
[24]*The Art of Illustration, op. cit.,* p. 21.
[25]A. W. Blackwood, *The Preparation of Sermons,* p. 37. New York: Nashville: Abingdon-Cokesbury Press, 1948.

angel fly by me, and hear the horsehoofs of the Cherubim as they dashed along the stony road when I have been out preaching the Word.[26]

Realistic Description

Finally, the passage under consideration beautifully exhibits the best sort of description. Description is required to make another person see what the speaker has seen in the way that he has synthesized it. It is likely that many of Spurgeon's hearers did not know of the tremendous numbers of bacteria which fill the air. Could they fail to realize this after Spurgeon described the very air around them ("this air") as "dense" with animalculae? God uses means to feed the animal creation, but the very use of these means tends to obscure man's view of God's activity in providence. Spurgeon wanted his hearers to get a "View of God's Glory" (a topic that is charged with Sense Appeal[27]). Therefore, he spoke not of the fields ripe with birdseed, but of the ravens coming to "peck their food from His liberal hands."

Two factors comprise the essence of Spurgeon's descriptive powers. First, vivid, descriptive vocabulary and phraseology abound. Spurgeon was conscious of the importance of words. He once said, "How frequently a word in itself is a picture."[28] Such picture words as "dance, feathered songsters, quiver, atom, dense, peck, hands, leap, roars" conjure up mental scenes which otherwise might have remained dormant in the memory. Dale could have been describing Spurgeon when he said,

> The imaginative speaker instinctively rejects words, phrases, symbols, which are incapable of being animated with vital warmth.[29]

In his *Lectures,* Spurgeon advised his students, "Our hearers do not want the bare bones of definition, but meat and flavor."[30] Perhaps, this sense appealing word "flavor" most aptly characterizes the relationship live words bear to description. They truly may be said to "flavor" it.

---

[26]Vol. 2, p. 192. Notice the appeal to his own two senses.
[27]See Appendix II for a discussion of Sense Appeal in the Topics and Texts of Spurgeon's Sermons.
[28]*The Art of Illustration,* p. 129.
[29]Dale, *op. cit.,* p. 47.
[30]*Op. cit.,* p. 219.

The second factor is mentioned by C. H. Pattison; the clarity of simplicity:

> But the effect was intensified by a choice of words, which, as in the case of John Bright also, were capable of one, and only one meaning.[31]

Brastow adds his confirmation, "he is one of the clearest of preachers."[32] The list of words, compiled from the passage considered above, without exception, contains terms of this sort. "Simple vividness" seems to epitomize Spurgeon's style of Realistic Description.

Spurgeon, however, would have preferred to describe Description itself! He would not be satisfied with my analytical approach. He once did so in a sermon entitled, "Christ Crucified":

> God gives his ministers a brush, and shows them how to use it in painting life-like portraits, and thus the sinner hears the special call.[33]

These words of his best summarize the role and method of the descriptive element in Sense Appeal, as he conceived of it. It is something that *God uses.*

The conclusion to be drawn from this analysis, in conjunction with the previous Chapter, is that Sense Appeal is the product of hard work, in which the powers of Perception, Imagination, and Description must be studiously and consciously trained through reading and exercise. There seems to be no easy method that may be used as a short cut. Primarily, the power of Sense Appeal will emerge from a study of literature that abounds in it, and in no other way.

---

[31] *The History of Christian Preaching,* p. 336. Philadelphia: The American Baptist Publication Society, 1903.
[32] *Op. cit.,* p. 395.
[33] Vol. I, p. 102. Spurgeon was a true Calvinist, always maintaining the proper balance between Divine sovereignty and human responsibility. This is why he stressed Effectual Calling, but not apart from, the means.

CHAPTER NINE
SUMMARY AND CONCLUSIONS

Conclusions

Little more needs to be said. The evidence for the existence of Sense Appeal is conclusive. Spurgeon's ability has been determined to stem more largely from hard work than from innate powers, thereby opening the same door to all others who will apply themselves to the same sort of study with similar diligence. The constituent elements of Sense Appeal, and the means of effectively employing it have been described in didactic principles, accessible to all.

Direct appeal should be mentioned again since Spurgeon was one of the few masters of its use, and at the present time there is so little of it.

A larger development of appeal to the senses of touch, taste, and smell may be urged as a goal for which others might strive. Spurgeon's own appeal to these senses though remarkably frequent still fell far below that of sight and hearing.

The study uncovered at least one area in which further work needs to be done, namely the relationship between the writings of John Bunyan and the sermons of Charles H. Spurgeon.

Summary

1. Spurgeon's sermons contain a noteworthy amount of Sense Appeal.
2. Spurgeon's ability to appeal to the senses was acquired primarily from a study of sermons (especially Puritan preachers in general, and John Bunyan in particular), an intensive study of nature, and of the whole sense realm.
3. Sense Appeal is of two sorts: Direct and Indirect.

4. The constituent elements of Sense Appeal are three: Perception, Imagination, and Description.
5. Effective Sense Appeal requires the equal development and functioning of each of these three elements, in complete harmony with one another, as they did in Spurgeon.

APPENDIX I

A COMPLETE ANALYSIS OF SENSE APPEAL IN SPURGEON'S SERMON,

"SONGS IN THE NIGHT"

The following sermon analysis was made from the printing of it in Andrew W. Blackwood's, *The Protestant Pulpit,* pp. 114-127. This publication was preferred to the one in the *Memorial Library,* because in Blackwood's edition the paragraphs are numbered.

The sermon, as Blackwood numbered them, contains thirty paragraphs. However, for the purposes of this study, these may be reduced to twenty-six. This is legitimate since four paragraphs (5,10,19,24) are nothing more than transitional paragraphs, one sentence long. In such a short compass, with material of that nature, one could not expect to encounter any Sense Appeal. Figuring then, that there are twenty-six true paragraphs, here are the results of the analysis:

1. There is no paragraph that does not contain an appeal to at least one of the senses.
2. Most paragraphs contain many references, either to the same sense, or distinct ones.
3. The total number of paragraphs containing references to

Sight—25 paragraphs (that is, sight appeal occurs in 25 of 26 possible paragraphs, although far more frequently than 25 times). The one paragraph (no. 22) in which no sight appeal appears is the shortest paragraph (with the exception of the four transitional sentences) in the sermon, consisting of but two sentences. Hearing appeal does occur in it, however.

Hearing—20 paragraphs. Of course, some allowance must be made for the high frequency of hearing appeal in this sermon since the text and title are based upon it. Only six paragraphs do not contain references.

Touch—7 paragraphs.

Taste—3 paragraphs.

Smell—0 references.

It is obvious from this summary that Sense Appeal plays a large part in the sermons of C. H. Spurgeon. This sermon is typical, and not extraordinary in this respect. The ratio of references to the various senses runs true to form, although the last three are usually of higher frequency, the last occurring almost as often as the fourth. All in all, then, this sermon analysis presents a good illustration of the whole.

APPENDIX II

SENSE APPEAL IN SPURGEON'S SERMON TITLES

Titles with Sense Appeal are of two sorts. First, there are those in which the element of Sense Appeal was originally part of the text, and in which it has been incorporated into the title with little or no alteration. An example of this is Spurgeon's, "Songs in the Night." Here the title is borrowed entirely from the Scriptures without modification. It contains Sight Appeal ("Night" arouses mental images of darkness, etc.) and Sound Appeal ("Songs"), both of which Spurgeon exploits to the limit in the sermon.

Secondly, there are titles into which the element of Sense Appeal has been engrafted from another source as from, for example, some illustration within the sermon. An illustration of this second sort is "The Enchanted Ground."

Of the four hundred and twenty-five sermon titles in the Memorial Library, at least one hundred and thirty-five unquestionably employ Sense Appeal. This is nearly one third. Some of the more impressive of these are as follows:

"The Enchanted Ground"

"Songs in the Night"

"A View of God's Glory"

"Light at Evening Time"

"The Voice of the Blood of Christ"

"The Dew of Christ's Youth"

"The Sight of Iniquity"

"A Frail Leaf"

"Black Clouds and Bright Blessings"

"Hands Full of Honey"

"Shaven and Shorn, but Not Beyond Hope"

Sometimes, Sense Appeal may be drawn from a text although the title itself contains no traces of it. For example, one message, entitled simply "Heaven and Hell," which was based upon Matthew 8:11-12, is constructed upon two very vivid contrasting word-descriptions found in the text itself. Spurgeon, in the introduction to this sermon says, "I like that text, because it tells me what heaven is, and gives me a beautiful picture of it." The remainder of the sermon is but an enlargement of these two pictures. But one would never know this from the title alone.

That Sense Appeal had some prominence in Spurgeon's titles readily may be seen, but it does not appear to the extent that one might have expected. It must be regretted that a man with his trained ability to perceive, synthesize and describe the sense realm did not always take the same care in composing titles as he sometimes did. For the most part, the titles are drab and unsuggestive, not at all portending the good things within the sermons themselves.

BIBLIOGRAPHY

Blackwood, Andrew W., *Biographical Preaching for Today.* New York: Abingdon Press, 1954.

—————., *Preaching from the Bible.* New York: Abingdon Press, 1941.

—————., *Preaching from the Prophetic Books.* New York: Abingdon Press, 1942.

—————., *The Preparation of Sermons* New York-Nashville: Abingdon-Cokesbury Press, 1948.

—————., *Imagination in Preaching in the New Schaff-Herzog Religious Encyclopedia,* Vol. I. Grand Rapids: Baker Book House, 1955.

—————., *The Protestant Pulpit.* New York-Nashville: Abingdon Press, 1957.

Brastow, Lewis O., *Representative Modern Preachers.* New York: Hodder and Stoughton, 1904.

—————., *The Modern Pulpit.* London: Macmillan, 1906.

Broadus, John A., *Preparation and Delivery of Sermons,* 41st edition. New York: George H. Doran Co., 1898.

Brown, John, *Puritan Preaching in England.* New York: Charles Scribner's Sons, 1900.

Cadman, S. Parkes, *Ambassadors of God.* New York: Macmillan, 1924.

Curry, S. S., *Vocal and Literary Interpretation of the Bible.* New York: Hodder and Stoughton, 1903.

Dargan, Edwin Charles, *A History of Preaching,* Vol. I. Grand Rapids: Baker Book House, 1954.

Davis, Ozora S., *Principles of Preaching*. Chicago: University of Chicago Press, 1924.

Fullerton, W. Y., *C. H. Spurgeon, A Biography*. London: 1920.

Garrison, Webb. B., *The Preacher and His Audience*. Westwood, N. J.: Fleming H. Revell, 1954.

Garvie, Alfred Ernest, *The Christian Preacher*. New York: Charles Scribner's Sons, 1921.

Howard, Harry C., *Princes of the Christian Pulpit and Pastorate*. Nashville: Cokesbury Press, 1927.

Hoyt, Arthur S., *The Work of Preaching*. New York: Macmillan, 1956.

Jefferson, Charles Edward, *The Ministering Shepherd*. Paris: Y.M.C.A., no date.

Jones, Ilion T., *Principles and Practice of Preaching*. New York: Abingdon Press, 1956.

Lorimer, George C., *Charles Haddon Spurgeon, The Puritan Preacher*. Boston: Jas. H. Earle, Publisher, 1892.

Macpherson, Ian, *The Burden of the Lord*. New York-Nashville: Abingdon Press, 1955.

Magoon, E. L., *The Modern Whitfield*. New York: Sheldon, Blakeman and Co., 1856.

Needham, George C., *Charles H. Spurgeon His Life and Labors*. Manchester, Mass.: Albert Needham Pub., 1890.

Nicholl, W. Robertson, *Princes of the Church*, 4th edition. London: Hodder and Stoughton, 1921.

Page, Jesse, *C. H. Spurgeon, His Life and Ministry*. New York: Fleming H. Revell, no date.

Pattison, C. Harwood, *The History of Christian Preaching*. Philadelphia: American Baptist Publication Society, 1903.

Sangster, E. W., *The Craft of Sermon Illustration*. Philadelphia: Westminster Press, 1950.

Shindler, Robert, *From the Usher's Desk to the Tabernacle Pulpit.* New York: A. C. Armstrong and Son, 1893.

Spurgeon, Charles H., *An All-Round Ministry.* London: Passmore and Alabaster, 1900.

—————., *The Art of Illustration.* New York: Wilbur B. Ketcham, 1894.

—————., *Flashes of Thought.* London: Passmore and Alabaster, 1888.

—————., *The Gospel of the Kingdom.* New York: Baker, 1893.

—————., *Illustrations and Meditations.* New York: Funk and Wagnalls, 1883.

—————., *Lectures to my Students.* New York: American Tract Society, no date.

—————., *Second Series of Lectures to my Students.* New York: Robert Carter and Brothers, 1889.

—————., *Great Pulpit Masters,* Vol. II. Introduction by Andrew W. Blackwood. New York: Fleming H. Revell Co., 1949.

—————., *Spurgeon's Sermons,* (Memorial Library) 20 volumes. New York: Funk and Wagnalls Co., no date.

—————., *Autobiography of Charles H. Spurgeon,* edited by his wife and secretary, 4 volumes. Chicago: Fleming H. Revell and Co., 1898.

Wayland, H. L., *Charles H. Spurgeon: His Faith and Works.* Philadelphia: American Baptist Publication Society, 1892.

Webber, F. R., *A History of Preaching,* Part I. Milwaukee: Northwestern Publishing House, 1952.

Wilkinson, Wm. Cleaver, *Modern Masters of Pulpit Discourse.* New York: Funk and Wagnalls, 1905.